Mary Jones, Diane Fellowes-Freeman and Michael Smyth

Cambridge Checkpoint
Science

Challenge Workbook

7

CAMBRIDGE
UNIVERSITY PRESS

University Printing House, Cambridge CB2 8BS, United Kingdom

One Liberty Plaza, 20th Floor, New York, NY 10006, USA

477 Williamstown Road, Port Melbourne, VIC 3207, Australia

314–321, 3rd Floor, Plot 3, Splendor Forum, Jasola District Centre,
New Delhi – 110025, India

79 Anson Road, #06–04/06, Singapore 079906

Cambridge University Press is part of the University of Cambridge.

It furthers the University's mission by disseminating knowledge in the pursuit of
education, learning and research at the highest international levels of excellence.

www.cambridge.org
Information on this title: www.cambridge.org/9781316637197 (Paperback)

© Cambridge University Press 2017

First published 2017

20 19 18 17 16 15 14 13 12 11 10 9 8 7 6 5 4

Printed in Great Britain by CPI Group (UK) Ltd, Croydon CR0 4YY

A catalogue record for this publication is available from the British Library

ISBN 978-1-316-63719-7 Paperback

Produced for Cambridge University Press by White-Thomson Publishing
www.wtpub.co.uk
Editor: Rachel Minay
Designer: Clare Nicholas

All Checkpoint-style questions and sample answers within this workbook are
written by the authors.

Acknowledgements

The authors and publishers acknowledge the following sources for photographs:

Cover Pal Hermansen/Steve Bloom Images/Alamy Stock Photo; 3.01 Woods Hole
Oceanographic Institution, Visuals Unlimited/Science Photo Library; 4.01 by kind
permission of Seshadri K.S/ 8.01a CribbVisuals/Getty Images; 8.01b Unidentified/Getty
Images; 8.01c VvoeVale/Getty Images; 11.02 Royal Astronomical Society/Science Photo
Library; 11.03 NASA/JPL/Science Photo Library

....

Contents

Introduction

Welcome to the Cambridge Checkpoint Science Challenge Workbook 7

The Cambridge Checkpoint Science course covers the Cambridge Secondary 1 Science curriculum framework. The course is divided into three stages: 7, 8 and 9.

You should use this Challenge Workbook with Coursebook 7 and Workbook 7. The tasks in this Challenge Workbook will help you to develop and extend your skills and understanding in science. This workbook is offered as an extension to the main curriculum and therefore it does not cover all the curriculum framework content for this stage.

The tasks will challenge you with scientific enquiry skills, such as planning investigations, interpreting and analysing results, forming conclusions and discussing them.

They will also challenge you to **apply** your knowledge to answer questions that you have not seen before, rather than just recall that knowledge.

If you get stuck with a task:

Read the question again and look carefully at any diagrams to find any clues.

Think carefully about what you already know **and** how you can use it in the answer.

Look up any words you do not understand in the glossary at the back of the Checkpoint Science Coursebook, or in your dictionary.

Read through the matching section in the Coursebook. Look carefully at the diagrams there too.

Check the reference section at the back of the Coursebook. There is a lot of useful information there.

Introducing the learners

Nor

Amal

Sam

Anna

Elsa

Jon

1.1 Comparing plant structures

This challenge task relates to **1.1 Plant organs** from the Coursebook.

In this challenge task, you will practise writing clear, simple descriptions. You will then make a comparison between two plants.

1 Use your own words to outline the functions of:

leaves ....

flowers ....

roots ....

stems ....

For the next question, look at the diagrams of two plants.

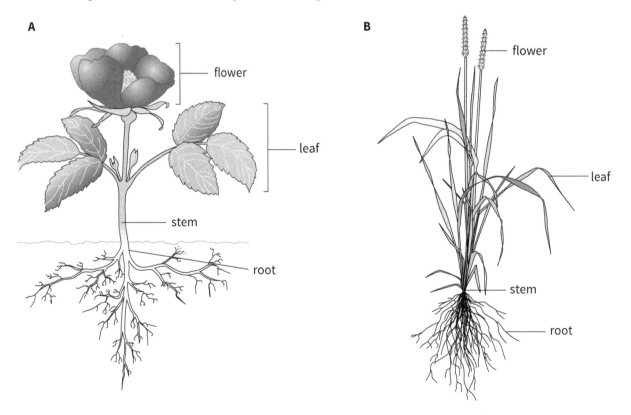

2 Construct a table to **compare** the structures of the two plants on the previous page. Try to include at least **ten** differences in your table.

Draw the table using a ruler and a pencil.

Keep comparable points opposite one another.

Draw horizontal lines between each set of points.

1.2 Choosing a question about bones to investigate

This challenge task relates to **1.3 The human skeleton** from the Coursebook.

> In this challenge task, you will choose a suitable question that can be answered by experiment, and then plan the experiment.

The diagram shows apparatus that can be used to answer this question:

Do long bones break more easily than short bones?

1 Here are some more questions about bones.
   Tick the **two** questions that could be investigated using the method shown in the diagram.

   Are thick bones stronger than thin bones? ☐

   Do people who eat plenty of calcium have stronger bones than people who do not? ☐

   Do old bones break more easily than young bones? ☐

   Do hollow bones break more easily than solid bones? ☐

pull

forcemeter

straw

2 Choose **one** of the questions that you have ticked in question 1.

   Write the question here:

   ....

   Plan an experiment to try to answer your chosen question. Your experiment must use the method shown in the diagram.

   a What will you change in your experiment?

   ....

   b What will you measure to collect your results?

   ....

   c What will you try to keep the same?

   ....

   ....

   ....

   ....

d Describe clearly how you will carry out your experiment.

....

....

....

....

....

....

....

....

e Draw a results chart that you could use. Include headings and units.

f Predict what you expect to find in your experiment.

....

....

....

Your teacher may allow you to carry out your experiment.

If so, you will probably find that you want to make some changes to your plan once you are actually doing it.

That is a good thing – scientists always try to improve their plans for experiments.

1.3 Planning an experiment about muscles

This challenge task relates to **1.5 Muscles** from the Coursebook.

> This challenge task will help you to improve your skills in planning your own experiment.

The biceps is the strongest muscle in your arm. When the biceps contracts, the arm bends at the elbow.

When you lift a weight as shown in the diagram, your biceps muscle produces the force to lift the weight.

You can investigate how quickly your biceps muscle gets tired, by counting how many times you can lift a weight in one minute over a period of several consecutive minutes.

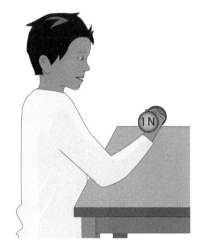

Rest your lower arm on a table top. Lift the weight using only the lower arm. Try not to bend your wrist.

1 Plan an experiment to answer this question:

Does the biceps muscle get tired more quickly after a person has been jumping than after they have been sitting still?

Try to write your plan very clearly, so that someone else could follow it to do your experiment.

> You can use questions 2 a–f in Challenge 1.2 to help you to structure your plan.

....

....

....

....

....

....

....

....

....

....

....

....

....

....

....

....

....

....

....

....

....

....

....

....

....

2.1 Analysing data about mould on bread

This challenge task relates to **2.3 Micro-organisms and decay** from the Coursebook.

> In this challenge task, you will use results from an experiment to construct a line graph, analyse the results and make a conclusion. You will also use information to suggest an explanation.

Jon and Amal investigated how temperature affects the growth of mould on moist bread.

They took some slices of bread and cut them into 15 equal-sized pieces. They placed three pieces in each of five identical dishes. One of the dishes is shown in the diagram.

The boys added the same volume of water to each dish – just enough to make sure the bread was damp.

They then placed the dishes in five containers, each kept at a different temperature, ranging from –4 °C to 60 °C. They left the dishes in the containers for three days. Each day, they added a small volume of water to each dish to keep the bread damp.

On the fourth day, the boys measured the area of the bread that had mould growing on it. Their results are shown in the table.

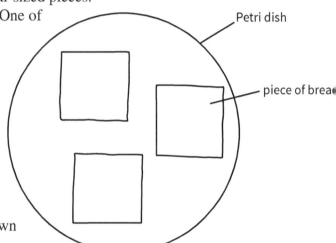

Petri dish

piece of bread

Dish	Temperature in °C	Area of mould growth in mm²			
		Bread sample 1	Bread sample 2	Bread sample 3	Mean
1	–4	0	1	0	0.3
2	10	2	3	3	2.7
3	20	12	8	9	9.7
4	40	14	5	18	
5	60	10	12	13	

1 Suggest how the boys could **estimate** the area of mould growing on the bread.

    ....

    ....

    ....

2 One of the results for the dish kept at 40 °C does not fit the pattern of all the other results. Draw a circle around the result that does not fit.

3 Ignoring the result you have circled, calculate the **mean** area of mould growth for the dishes kept at 40 °C.

To do this, add up the other two results and divide by 2. Write your answer in the table on the previous page.

> When you write numbers to one decimal place:
>
> 32.48 becomes 32.5
>
> 32 becomes 32.0

4 Calculate the mean area of mould growth in the dish kept at 60 °C. Write your answer to **one decimal place**. Write your answer in the table.

5 Construct a line graph on the grid, showing the mean area of mould growth at different temperatures.

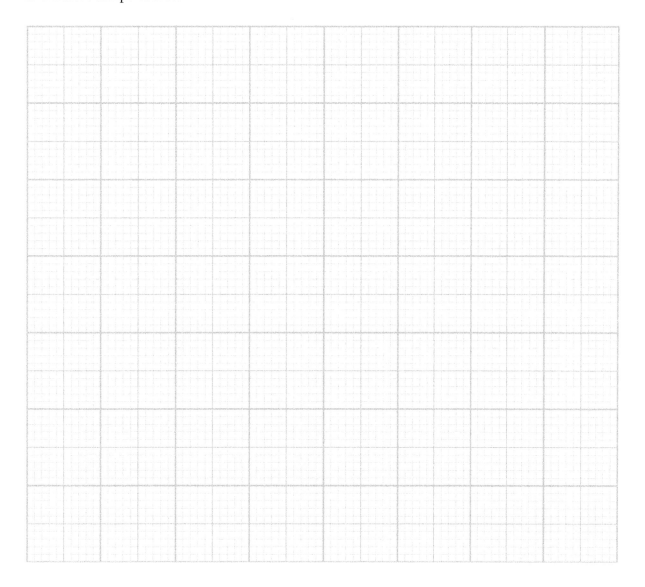

6 Suggest why the results for the three bread samples at a particular temperature are not exactly the same.

....

....

....

7 Use the boys' results to make a **conclusion**.

....

....

....

8 Jon found some information on the internet:

> All cells, including micro-organisms, are kept alive by chemical reactions that happen inside the cells. The faster the reactions happen, the faster the micro-organism grows and reproduces.
>
> Chemical reactions happen faster when it is warm than when it is cold. The reactions take place very slowly, or not at all, at low temperatures, but speed up at higher temperatures. However, at very high temperatures, the reactions stop.

> It is very important to use your own words in your explanation. You must not copy sentences that have been taken from the internet or a book.

Use the information that Jon found to suggest an **explanation** for the boys' results.

....

....

....

....

....

....

....

....

....

2.2 Stinging cells in *Hydra*

This challenge task relates to **2.7 Animal cells** and **2.8 Cells, tissues and organs** from the Coursebook.

> In this challenge task, you will practise finding relevant information in text and diagrams. You will then apply this information, and your knowledge of cells, tissues and organs, to answer questions.

Hydra is a tiny animal that lives in freshwater ponds. It has tentacles that it uses to catch even smaller animals, which it pushes into its mouth. The mouth opens into a cavity where digestion takes place.

The body of a *Hydra* is made up of two layers of cells. The diagram shows what a *Hydra* would look like if you sliced one in two from top to bottom and looked at it through a microscope.

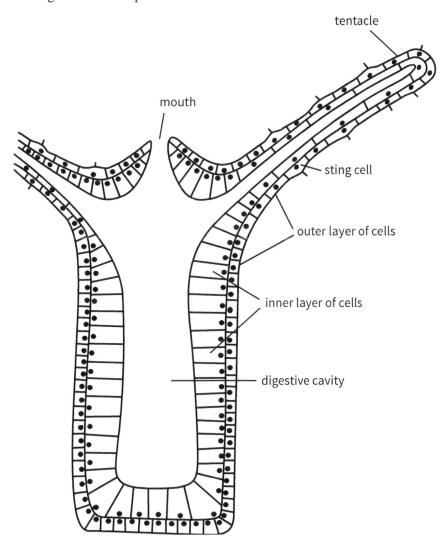

Hydra has some specialised cells called sting cells to help it to catch its food. These cells contain tiny coiled threads. When a prey animal touches the trigger on the sting cell, the thread shoots out and wraps around the prey. Some of these threads may have poisonous chemicals on them, which kill the prey. The diagram shows a sting cell before and after it has been triggered.

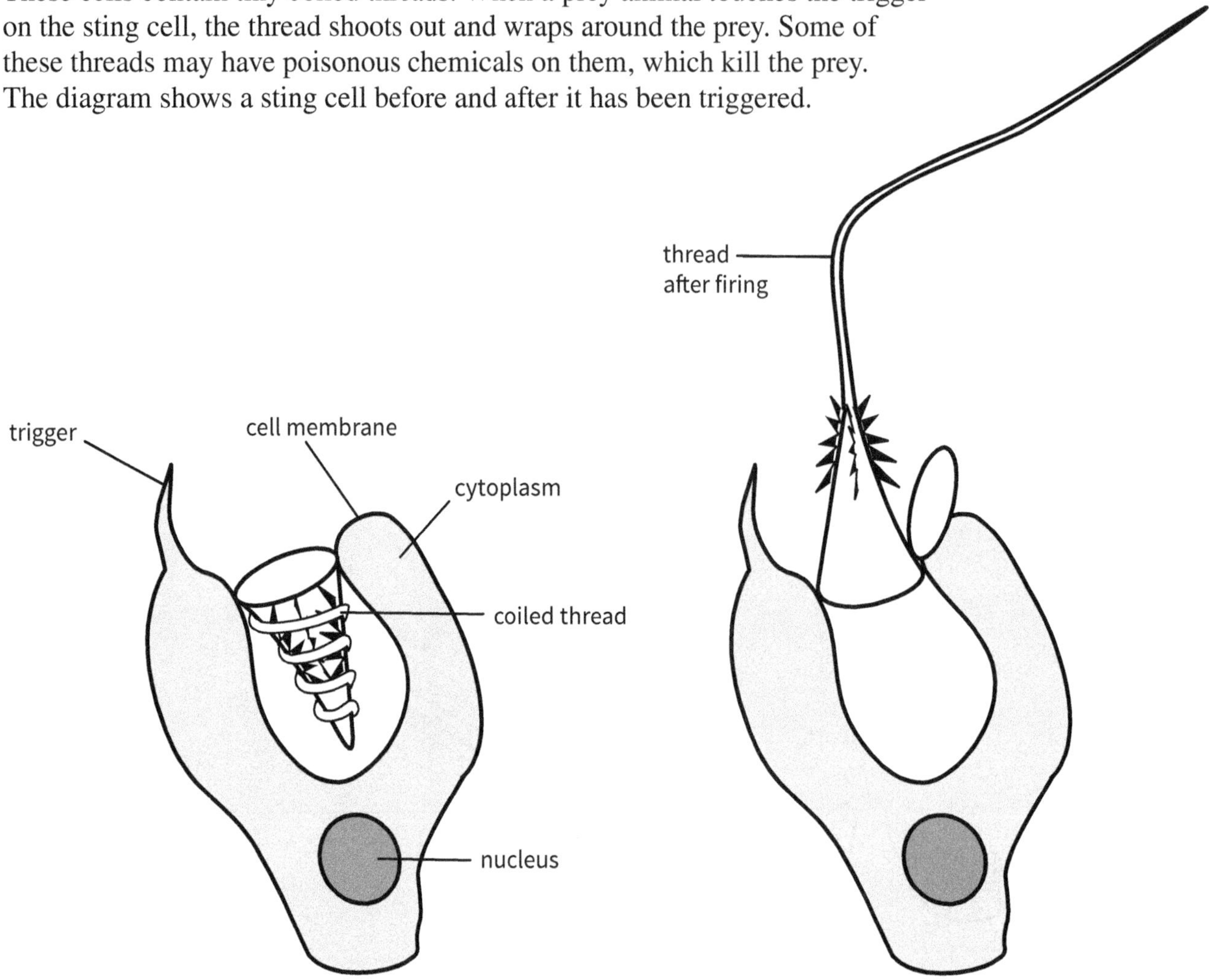

thread after firing

trigger

cell membrane

cytoplasm

coiled thread

nucleus

1 For each of these parts of a *Hydra*, decide whether it is a **cell**, a **tissue** or an **organ**.

   a inner layer of cells ....

   b outer layer of cells ....

   c sting cell ....

   d tentacle ....

2 In humans, there are several different organs that make up the digestive system.

   Does *Hydra* have a digestive system? Explain your answer.

   ....

   ....

   ....

3 List **three** features of a sting cell that you would expect to find in most animal cells.

....

....

....

4 Explain how you can tell from the diagram that the sting cell is an animal cell and not a plant cell.

....

....

....

5 A sting cell is a specialised cell. In your own words, explain how a sting cell is adapted for its function.

....

....

....

....

....

....

....

....

....

....

....

....

3.1 Hydrothermal vents

This challenge task relates to **3.2 Food chains** from the Coursebook.

> In this challenge task, you will interpret information about a very unusual food chain.

Hydrothermal vents are places in the ocean floor where hot water pours out into the sea water. These vents are often at depths of over 2000 m.

Scientists first discovered hydrothermal vents in 1977. They were amazed to find that many different kinds of micro-organisms and animals lived around them. They had not expected to find any life, because there is no light at that depth, so there are no plants that can form the start of a food chain. And the water that pours out of the vents is very hot, often up to 400 °C. The water cools rapidly as you go further from the vent.

We now know that, instead of plants, tiny bacteria are the starting point of the food chain at a hydrothermal vent. These bacteria use energy in the chemicals that flow out from the hot water vents to make food.

Some of these bacteria live inside giant tube worms. The food that the bacteria make is used by the worms. Other bacteria live in the hot water around the vent. These are eaten by shrimps and tiny floating animals called zooplankton. The zooplankton are eaten by sea anemones and mussels. Octopuses eat sea anemones and tube worms.

Giant tube worms at a hydrothermal vent

1 Explain why plants cannot live around a hydrothermal vent.

....

....

....

....

2 None of the organisms that live around hydrothermal vents has eyes.
Suggest why this is.

....

....

3 Construct **one** food chain, containing **four** types of organism, that occurs at
a hydrothermal vent.

4 Name the producer in your food chain. ....

5 Where does this producer obtain its energy from? ....

6 List all of the consumers in your food chain.

....

....

7 How is your food chain similar to a food chain that you would find on land?

....

....

....

....

8 What is the major difference between your food chain and a food chain that
you would find on land?

....

....

3.2 Water pollution in Bangladesh

This challenge task relates to **3.4 Pollution** from the Coursebook.

> In this challenge task, you will draw a line graph with three lines on the same pair of axes. You will then combine information from your graphs, and another graph, to work out a possible explanation for the patterns in a set of results.

Dhaka is the capital city of Bangladesh. Several rivers flow through Dhaka. These rivers are polluted by untreated sewage. Scientists in Dhaka wanted to find out if the effects of pollution in three of the rivers vary at different times of year.

One of the ways in which the scientists measured the effects of pollution was to find the concentration of dissolved oxygen in the water. Water that is polluted with untreated sewage has less dissolved oxygen. This is because bacteria in the water can feed on the sewage, and reproduce quickly. This produces large populations of bacteria, which use up a lot of the oxygen from the water as they respire.

The table shows the scientists' results. They did not make any measurements in September, October, January or June.

Month	Concentration of dissolved oxygen in mg per dm³		
	River Turag	**River Buriganga**	**River Shitalakkhya**
August	3.3	3.5	4.0
September			
October			
November	1.5	1.7	1.0
December	1.0	1.8	1.3
January			
February	0.9	1.7	0.6
March	1.1	1.9	1.5
April	0.4	1.4	2.0
May	0.5	0.5	2.6
June			
July	0.7	1.9	3.8

1 Draw a line graph to show the results in the table on the previous page.

Plot a separate line on the graph for each river.

Use a ruler and pencil to draw straight lines from one point to the next.

> It might be helpful to look at the graph on the next page. Put **month** on the *x*-axis. Put **concentration of dissolved oxygen** on the *y*-axis.

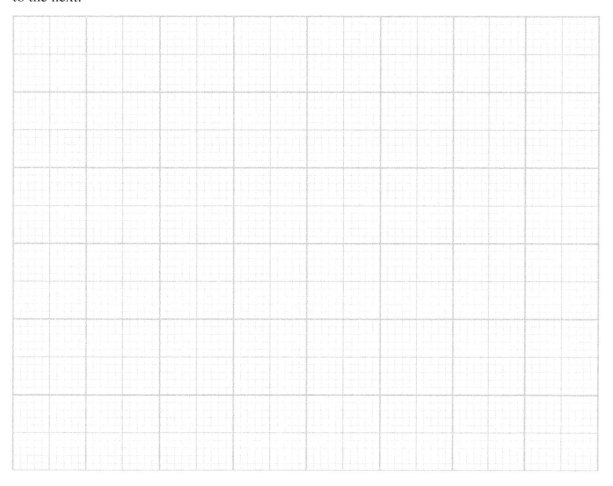

2 Which river had the lowest reading for the concentration of dissolved oxygen? What was this oxygen concentration? (Remember to include units in your answer.)

....

3 In which month did all three rivers have the highest concentrations of dissolved oxygen?

....

4 In which month was the River Buriganga most polluted? Explain your answer.

....

....

....

....

> Read the information on the previous page to remind you what the concentration of dissolved oxygen tells us about the level of pollution.

The researchers also measured the volume of water flowing in each river.
They measured this in cubic metres per second. The graph shows their results.

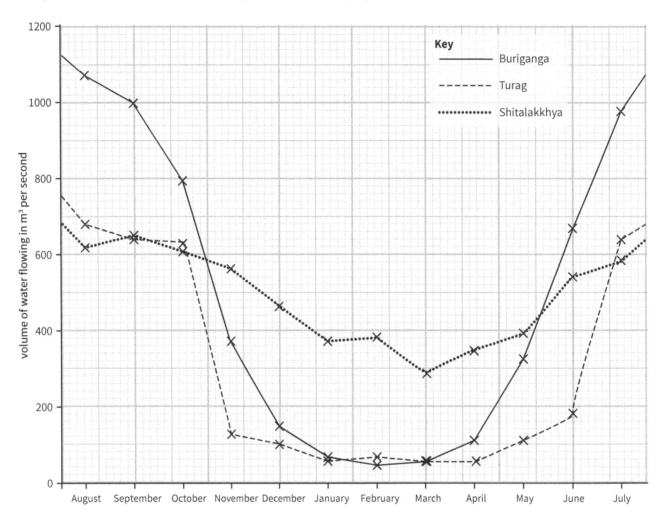

5 Bangladesh has distinct wet and dry seasons. Use the graph to identify when the dry season occurs in Bangladesh.

Tick **one** answer.

May to June ☐

June to November ☐

December to April ☐

6 Suggest how the changes in the volume of water flowing in the rivers could help to explain the patterns in the level of oxygen concentration over the year.

> This is not an easy question. You may like to discuss your ideas with a friend before you start to write.

....

....

....

....

....

....

....

....

....

....

....

....

....

3.3 Conserving snow leopards

This challenge task relates to **3.6 Conservation** from the Coursebook.

> In this challenge task, you will practise using information from several different sources to write a concise account in your own words. Use your dictionary if there are any words that you do not understand, or to help you to write your answers.

Snow leopards live in high mountains in central and southern Asia. The map shows the parts of the world where we think snow leopards are living.

Parts of the world where snow leopards may be found

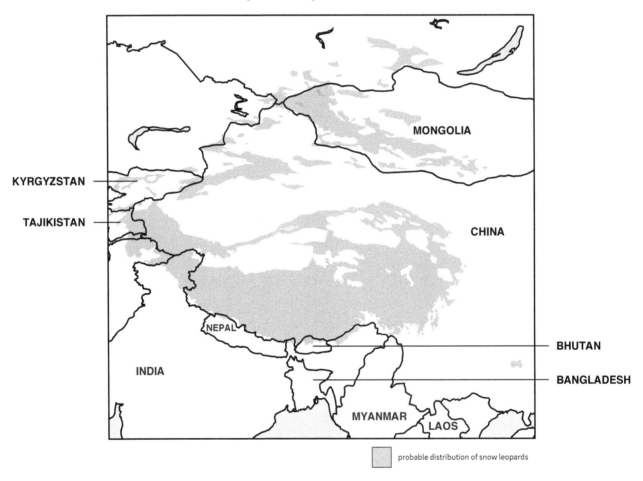

probable distribution of snow leopards

The number of snow leopards is falling rapidly. They will become extinct unless we try to conserve them. It is difficult to conserve snow leopards because they often live close to borders between countries that do not find it easy to co-operate with one another.

Snow leopards have no natural predators, except humans. Snow leopards take livestock from villages, so local people often want to reduce the numbers of snow leopards.

Researchers in Nepal carried out a study in Shey-Phoksundo National Park. They found out what the snow leopards ate, and how this affected the local people.

To find what the snow leopards ate, the researchers looked at 40 samples of snow leopard faeces that they found on the ground. They studied the faeces under the microscope, and identified hairs and bones from the animals the snow leopards had eaten. The pie chart shows the results.

What snow leopards eat

The researchers also investigated whether snow leopards really were a serious threat to livestock. They asked 250 households in the National Park to complete a questionnaire. They found that, on average, each household owned 33 animals, and that they lost three or four animals per year. The bar chart shows the causes of these losses of livestock.

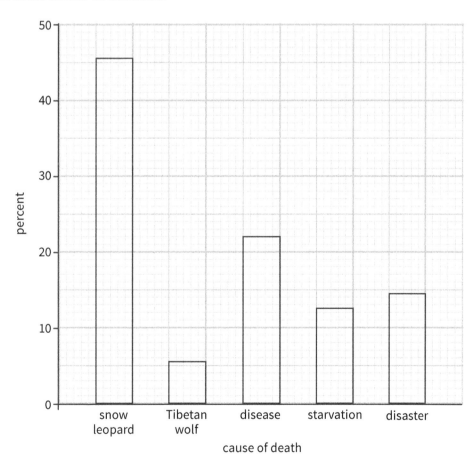

1 Use the information in the paragraphs, the map, the pie chart and the bar chart to write your own account of the problems affecting the conservation of snow leopards. You must use your own words.

Plan your answer carefully before you begin to write.

Here are some things you might like to include:

- why snow leopards need to be conserved

- why it is difficult to conserve snow leopards

- the evidence that the researchers found in their study, and how reliable you think this evidence might be

- your own ideas about what could be done to make it easier to conserve snow leopards in Shey-Phoksundo National Park.

....

....

....

....

....

....

....

....

....

....

....

....

....

....

....

....

....

....

....

....

Unit 4 Variation and classification

4.1 A new frog species

This challenge task relates to **4.1 What is a species?** from the Coursebook.

> In this challenge task, you will use your understanding of what makes a separate species. You will suggest how scientists could decide how to classify a newly discovered kind of frog.

In 2016, a team of researchers from India and the National University of Singapore discovered an unusual frog in a rocky habitat near the coast of southwest India.

The frog is very tiny – only about 16 mm long. It looks similar to other little frogs that are classified in the group *Microhyla*. This frog is pale brown and has black and orangey-red markings on its back, feet and sides. The males make a call that sounds like a cricket chirping.

The researchers thought that the frog looked different from the eight species of *Microhyla* known to live in India. They thought it might be a new species, not known about before. They named it *Microhyla laterite*.

1 Suggest what the researchers should do to decide whether or not their frog really is a new species. You could think about these things:

- How many specimens of the new frog should they collect? (Think about how much evidence they need, as well as the fact that this species might be rare.)

- What evidence should the researchers collect?

- How should the researchers use this evidence to make a decision about whether or not the frog belongs to a new species?

> You could research information about the discovery of *Microhyla laterite* on the internet. You could add some of this information to your answer.

....

....

....

....

....

....

....

....

....

....

....

....

....

....

....

....

....

....

....

....

4.2 Variation in pea pods

This challenge task relates to **4.2 Variation in a species** and **4.3 Investigating variation** from the Coursebook.

> In this challenge task, you will choose a characteristic that shows variation in a plant species and decide how to record data about your chosen characteristic. You will then construct a frequency diagram.

The drawing shows 20 pea pods, opened to show the seeds inside.

1 List **three** features that show variation in these pea pods.

   ....

   ....

   ....

   ....

   ....

2 Choose **one** of the features in your list that you can assess by counting it or measuring it.

   Chosen feature...

   Count or measure this feature in each of the pea pods. Write your results in the space below.

3 Construct a **tally chart** in which you can record your results.

> You will probably need to group your results into **categories**. Try to have at least four categories, but no more than ten. Ask your teacher for help if you are not sure about this.

4 Use your results to construct a **frequency diagram**.

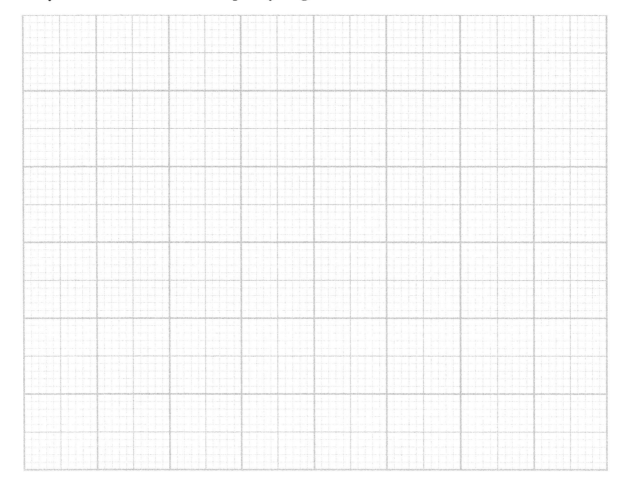

4.3 Researching a group of invertebrates

This challenge task relates to **4.6 Classifying invertebrates** from the Coursebook.

In this challenge task, you will research information about a group of invertebrates. You will then summarise and present your information in an interesting way.

Most people know something about molluscs, annelids and arthropods. But there are many other kinds of invertebrates that are much less familiar.

1 Your task is to choose **one** other group of invertebrates, research information about it, and then write a clear account of your findings.

Here are some suggestions for groups you might like to research.

Porifera (sponges)   **Cnidaria (sea anemones and jellyfish)**

Platyhelminthes (flatworms)   **Tardigrada (water bears)**

Echinodermata (starfish and sea urchins)

Use this space and the next page to present the information you have found.

Select the most useful and most interesting pieces of information.

Summarise the information **in your own words** and with labelled drawings.

....

....

....

....

....

....

....

....

....

....

....

4 Variation and classification

5.1 Properties of solids, liquids and gases

This challenge task relates to **5.1 States of matter** from the Coursebook.

> In this challenge task, you will consider some observations of unusual behaviour of a solid. Then you will discuss and explain the reasons for these observations.

Flour is a solid, but it is in powder form. When Jon was baking, he observed that the flour had the properties shown here.

A He poured it.

B He found it took the shape of the container.

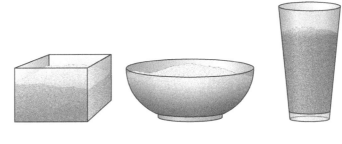

C When he tapped the container of flour on the table, the flour took up less space.

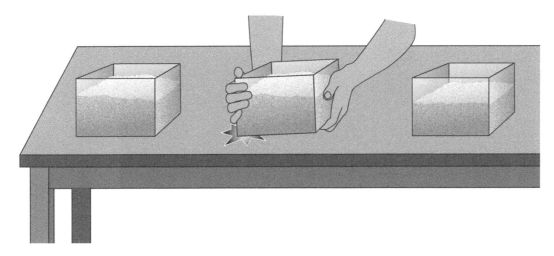

The properties shown in diagrams A, B and C on the previous page are not usually those of a solid.

1 Write down which state(s) of matter you would **expect** to have the property shown in:

A ....

B ....

2 **Explain** why the flour has the property shown in:

A ....

   ....

   ....

B ....

   ....

   ....

C ....

   ....

   ....

5.2 Investigating fizzy drinks

This challenge task relates to **5.1 States of matter** from the Coursebook.

> This challenge task will help you to develop your investigation skills.

When you open a bottle of a fizzy drink and leave it, it goes flat (loses its fizz) because the gas comes out of the drink. Think about what happens to the mass of the drink when the drink goes flat.

Read the **predictions** and **explanations** that the three students make.

A
Gases are lighter than air – that's why they float. Think about a balloon when the gas escapes: the balloon falls to the ground because it is heavier. So when the gas escapes, the drink will get heavier.

B
I think that gases do not have any mass, so it will not make any difference to the mass of the drink. The mass will stay the same.

C
The gas is escaping from the drink, so there is less 'stuff' in the bottle than at the start. It must get lighter.

1 Which prediction and explanation do you think is correct? Give reasons for your answer.

....

....

....

....

....

....

2 How could you investigate the prediction that you chose in question 1?

Write a method for your investigation.

Think about:
- How often will you take readings?
- For how long will you continue to take readings?
- How accurate does the balance need to be?

....

....

....

....

....

....

....

....

....

....

3 Draw a table to collect the results, to show how the mass of the drink changes with time.

5.3 Investigating hot liquids

This challenge task relates to **5.3 Changing state** from the Coursebook.

> This challenge task will give you practice in planning investigations, displaying results as a graph and making conclusions.

This investigation is to find out if oil gets runnier when it gets hotter.

Amal, Anna and Sam used the apparatus shown here.

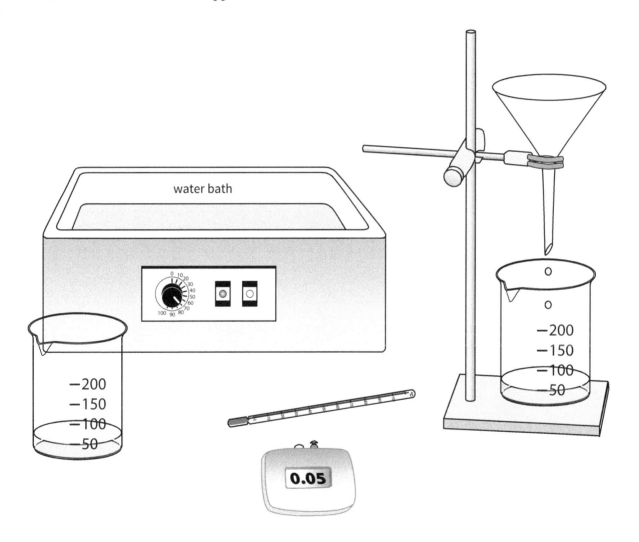

These are their results:

Oil temperature in °C	Time for oil to run through funnel in seconds			
	Amal's results	Anna's results	Sam's results	Mean
23	137	132	128	
30	55	57	54	
40	33	36	35	
50	27	25	24	
60	22	21	23	
70	18	20	19	
80	18	18	19	

1 If your teacher asked you to do this investigation using the apparatus shown, describe what you would do.

....

....

....

....

....

....

....

2 What did the students keep the same each time to make their investigation a fair test?

....

....

....

3 Suggest why the students' first test, the coolest one, was at 23 °C and not at 20 °C.

....

....

4 Calculate the **mean** time taken at each temperature and add the means to the table above.

Write your answers to **one decimal place**.

When you write numbers to one decimal place:

54.48 becomes 54.5

54 becomes 54.0

5 Plot a graph of the results. Put the temperature on the *x*-axis and time on the *y*-axis.

6 Write a conclusion for this investigation, which describes what Amal, Anna and Sam have found out.

....

....

....

....

....

5.4 Identifying anomalous results

This challenge task relates to **5.3 Changing state** from the Coursebook.

> This challenge task will help you to identify anomalous (unusual) experimental results and anomalous results on graphs.

Nor and Amal investigated heating water. The investigation was done in the same class and on the same day. Both students used the same volume of water, took water from the same tap, and heated the water for ten minutes. They used the apparatus shown here.

> Remember that time is the independent variable. The independent variable is always plotted on the *x*-axis.

The students got the results shown in the tables.

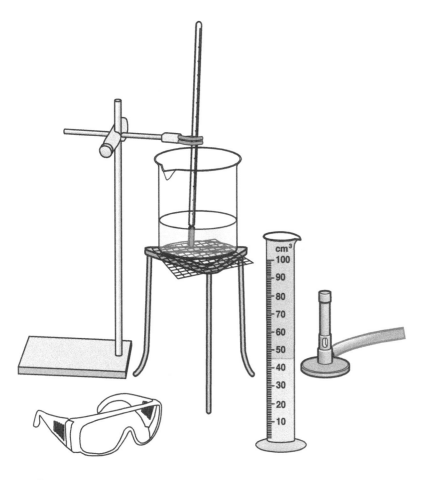

Nor's results

Time in minutes	Temperature in °C
0	20
1	25
2	32
3	32
4	48
5	58
6	65
7	70
8	77
9	70
10	86

Amal's results

Time in minutes	Temperature in °C
1	20
2	26
3	35
4	43
5	54
6	65
7	72
8	78
9	85
10	94

1 Explain which of Nor's readings do not fit the expected pattern. Look carefully at the readings in the table.

....

....

....

....

2 Suggest what Nor should do about these readings.

....

....

3 Amal's results seem to show a pattern, but what mistake has he made?

....

....

In a similar investigation, the following results were obtained. Graph A and graph B (on the next page) have been plotted from the same data.

Time in minutes	Temperature in °C
0	22
1	29
2	37
3	45
4	52
5	60
6	69
7	77
8	84
9	92
10	98

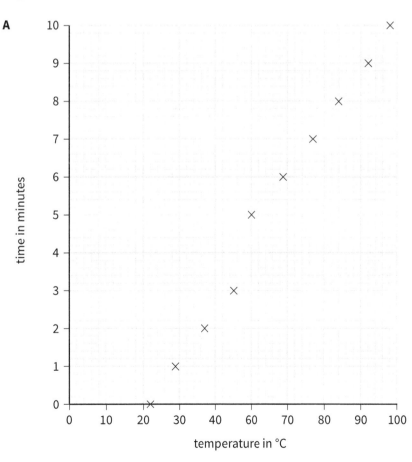

B

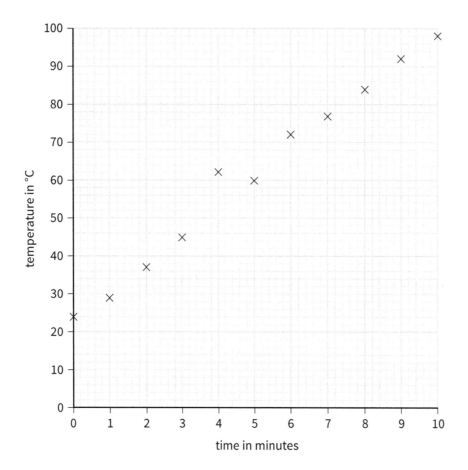

4 What mistakes have been made in graph A?

....

....

....

....

....

5 Draw circles around any points in graph B that have been plotted incorrectly.

> Remember to check the data from the table carefully.

Unit 6 Material properties

6.1 Properties of metals and non-metals

This challenge task relates to **6.3 Comparing metals and non-metals** from the Coursebook.

> In this challenge task, you will explain how to tell metals and non-metals apart by using their properties.

1 These words are useful when describing some materials. Explain what they mean.

   a ductile ....

   b brittle ....

   c malleable ....

2 Your teacher has given you a sample of a material you have never seen before. It is a grey solid.

   Which observations can you make and which investigations can you do to help you decide if it is a metal or a non-metal?

   Try to give at least **six** observations or investigations. Describe what you would expect these observations and investigations to tell you.

   ....

   ....

   ....

   ....

   ....

   ....

   ....

   ....

   ....

   ....

   ....

   ....

6.2 Identifying metals and non-metals

This challenge task relates to **6.3 Comparing metals and non-metals** from the Coursebook.

> In this challenge task, you will try to identify substances from information given.

Here is some information about six substances.

Substance A

It is a shiny liquid. The melting point is −39 °C. The boiling point is 357 °C. It conducts electricity. It is toxic.

Substance B

There are two forms of this substance; one is a black, dull, brittle and soft solid. This form conducts electricity. The other form is transparent, very hard and shiny. The melting point of the transparent form is 3730 °C.

Substance D

It is an unreactive gas with a melting point of −270 °C. It has a boiling point of −269 °C. It is very light. It does not conduct electricity.

Substance E

This is a reddish shiny solid. It conducts heat and electricity well. It has a melting point of 1082 °C and a boiling point of 2580 °C.

Substance C

It is a transparent gas with a melting point of −219 °C and a boiling point of −183 °C. It is essential for respiration in most living things. It does not conduct electricity.

Substance F

This is a yellow brittle solid that does not conduct electricity. The melting point is 119 °C and the boiling point is 445 °C.

1 For each substance:

- Decide if it is a metal or a non-metal, and give your reasons.

- Try to identify it.

- State a use for it.

> The melting points and boiling points will help you. You could use the internet to check your ideas and search for uses.

Substance A is a metal / non-metal.

My reason(s) for deciding this are: ....

....

I think that substance A is ....

One use for substance A is ....

Substance B is a metal / non-metal.

My reason(s) for deciding this are: ……………………………………………………………………

……

I think that substance B is ……………………………………………………………………………

One use for substance B is ……………………………………………………………………………

Substance C is a metal / non-metal.

My reason(s) for deciding this are: ……………………………………………………………………

……

I think that substance C is ……………………………………………………………………………

One use for substance C is ……………………………………………………………………………

Substance D is a metal / non-metal.

My reason(s) for deciding this are: ……………………………………………………………………

……

I think that substance D is ……………………………………………………………………………

One use for substance D is ……………………………………………………………………………

Substance E is a metal / non-metal.

My reason(s) for deciding this are: ……………………………………………………………………

……

I think that substance E is ……………………………………………………………………………

One use for substance E is ……………………………………………………………………………

Substance F is a metal / non-metal.

My reason(s) for deciding this are: ……………………………………………………………………

……

I think that substance F is ……………………………………………………………………………

One use for substance F is ……………………………………………………………………………

6.3 Choosing materials for a car

This challenge task relates to **6.4 Everyday materials and their properties** from the Coursebook.

> In this challenge task, you will use information from a table to compare the properties of some materials for a practical use – the bodywork of a car.

Read the paragraph below.

When cars were first produced, materials such as iron, steel, brass and wood were used. The first cars did not go very fast and were very heavy. These cars cost a lot of money. Each car was hand-built.

As cars developed, they became cheaper. Less expensive materials were used and the cars were produced in factories.

As time went on and fuel became more expensive, both the mass of the car and the amount of fuel it used became important issues.

Over the years, people have experimented with different materials for the bodywork of cars.

Three materials are being considered for use in a small car for driving around town.

Look at the information about the materials in the table on the next page.
Then answer the questions.

Feature	Material 1	Material 2	Material 3
Cost	expensive	cheap	very expensive
Mass	moderately heavy	very light	light
Availability	available from many local sources	available from a few specialist manufacturers; will need to be brought from a long distance away	available from many local sources
Ease of using the material to make the car	easy – this is a known technology	this is a new technology but very easy to work with	more care needed and workers will need more training
Effect of heat from the engine	expands slightly when heated, but not a problem	if exposed to high temperatures may buckle and deform	resistant to heat
Resistance to dents	dents easily	resistant to minor dents – the material 'bounces back'; it shatters if hit hard	strong material – dents only on high impact
Ease of repair to bodywork	easy to replace sections of bodywork; dents are knocked out easily	sections of bodywork can be replaced easily	sections of bodywork can be replaced, but workers will need training

1 Give one disadvantage of using each material for the car.

Material 1 ....

....

Material 2 ....

....

Material 3 ....

....

2 Give one advantage of using each material for the car.

Material 1 ....

....

Material 2 ....

....

Material 3 ....

....

3 Write a report on these materials, which would help the developers of this car make a decision about which, if any, to use.

Include any other information you think the developers will need to find out before they make a decision.

....

....

....

....

....

....

....

....

....

....

....

....

....

....

....

....

....

....

....

....

....

....

....

....

7.1 Key words for acids and alkalis

This challenge task relates to **7.1 Acids and alkalis**, **7.2 Is it an acid or an alkali?**, **7.3 The pH scale** and **7.4 Neutralisation** from the Coursebook.

> This challenge task will help you to learn the meanings of words about acids and alkalis.

1 Complete the table with the word or meaning.

Word	Meaning
	a substance with a pH of less than 7
neutralisation	
	able to dissolve or eat away other materials
alkali	
indicator	
	a mixture of different indicators that gives a range of colours in solutions of different pH
irritant	
	information found on bottles of chemicals to warn you of any dangers
pH scale	

7.2 Neutralising acid

This challenge task relates to **7.4 Neutralisation** from the Coursebook.

In this challenge task, you will identify some unsafe behaviour and mistakes made in a student's practical work with acids and alkalis, and suggest ways to correct these.

Your teacher is marking some homework. The class did some practical work on neutralisation and wrote an account of their work.

They were given these pieces of apparatus and chemicals.

One student has been away from school because he was ill for a week and has just handed this in. His report shows that he did not work safely.

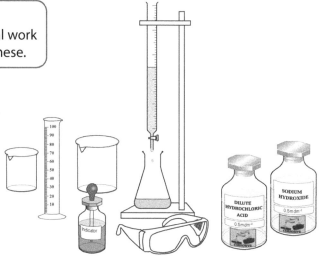

My practical work on neutralisation

I got on with my work quickly and went to get the chemicals.

I didn't wear the goggles because they hurt my nose.

Everyone was queuing to get the acid from the teacher.

This was marked 0.5 mol/dm³.

I didn't want to wait and there was another acid on the shelf behind the teacher's desk, so I used that – hydrochloric acid 1.0 mol/dm³.

I took the bottle to my desk and poured some in a beaker. It was about half full. I poured in about half a bottle of Universal Indicator. It went red.

I used the sodium hydroxide that the teacher put on the desk.

I added it straight into the beaker. I stirred it to see if it would go green, but it went blue at once.

So I added more acid and it went red. I tipped it all into a bigger beaker because there was too much liquid.

It was taking much too long, so I guessed how much alkali to use.

1 Write the correct method for neutralising acid, to show this student how the practical work should have been done.

You need to explain how to work safely at each step and use the correct names for equipment.

....

....

....

....

....

....

....

....

....

....

....

....

....

....

....

....

....

....

....

....

....

....

....

....

7.3 Transporting acid

This challenge task relates to **7.5 Neutralisation in action** from the Coursebook.

In this challenge task, you will present facts to explain the dangers of acids.

You are a news reporter and you have to report on a serious accident that happened on a major road. The accident involved a truck carrying concentrated acid. The emergency services attended the accident and dealt with the spill of acid.

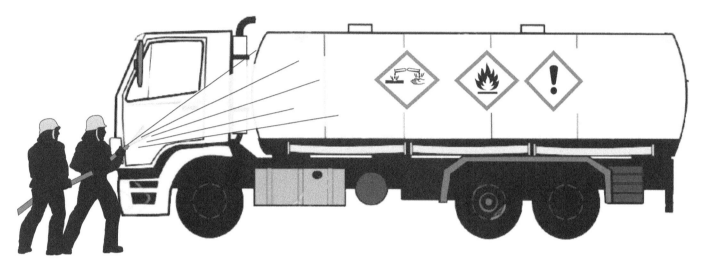

Before you write your report, answer the following questions. Then use your answers to help you write your report.

1 Why is the acid spill so dangerous?

....

....

2 What would happen if other people drove their cars through the acid spill?

....

....

3 How do the emergency services know which chemical they have to deal with?

....

....

4 What must the emergency services do to the spilt acid?

....

....

5 How will they know when the task is complete?

....

....

6 What safety measures must be taken by the emergency services while they deal with the spill?

....

....

7 In your news report, explain to the readers all of the points in your answers to questions 1–6. Suggest safety measures that should be in place when dangerous chemicals are transported on public roads.

> Tanker lorries must clearly display information about any dangerous materials in their loads. You could research the regulations.

....

....

....

....

....

....

....

....

....

....

....

....

....

....

....

....

....

7 Material changes

7.4 Investigating antacids

This challenge task relates to **7.6 Investigating acids and alkalis** from the Coursebook.

> This challenge task will help you to develop your scientific enquiry skills: using a table, plotting a graph and interpreting the results.

Sam and Nor investigate how effective medicines for indigestion are. They test five antacids to see how much acid they will neutralise.

They add 4 g of powdered antacid, 1 g at a time, to 25 cm³ of acid with a pH of 2. They check the pH after each addition of antacid with a pH meter.

A: pH 2, pH 3, pH 4, pH 5, pH 6
B: pH 2, pH 5, pH 7, pH 7, pH 7
C: pH 2, pH 2, pH 2, pH 3, pH 3
D: pH 2, pH 4, pH 6, pH 7, pH 7
E: pH 2, pH 2, pH 3, pH 3, pH 4

1 Write the results in the table.

Antacid powder	pH				
	after 0g	after 1g			

2 Plot the results from the table on the previous page as five different lines
on the graph below.

3 Which variables did Sam and Nor keep the same to make this a fair test?

....

....

4 Which antacid(s) had the biggest effect on the pH? ....

5 Which antacid(s) increased the pH most quickly? ....

6 Which antacid(s) had the least effect on the pH? ....

7 What pH would you expect if you added 2.5 g of powder B to the acid? ....

8 How much of powder A would you add to the acid to get a pH of 5.5? ....

9 The antacids that work very quickly produce a lot of gas quickly.

State which you would choose as the ideal antacid, and give your reasons.

....

....

....

8.1 Comparing rocks

This challenge task relates to **8.3 Igneous rocks**, **8.4 Sedimentary rocks** and **8.5 Metamorphic rocks** from the Coursebook.

> This challenge task will help you to compare the different types of rocks.

The three types of rocks are igneous, sedimentary and metamorphic. They have different structures, different properties, and are formed in different ways.

1 Compare the three types of rock by completing this table.

	Igneous
Give two examples of this type of rock.	....
How is this type of rock formed?	....
What is its structure? (Mention items such as grains, crystals, layers and fossils.)	....
Is this type of rock porous?	....
Is this type of rock hard or soft?	....
Does it react with acids?	....
What do we use this type of rock for, and why?	....

igneous   sedimentary   metamorphic

Sedimentary	Metamorphic
....	....
....	....
....	....
....	....
....	....
....	....
....	....
....	....
....	....
....	....
....	....
....	....
....	....
....	....
....	....

8.2 How rocks change

This challenge task relates to **8.7 Moving rocks** from the Coursebook.

> In this challenge task, you will read some written information about how rocks change, and then answer some questions. You may need to do some other reading and research.

Read this information.

Rocks are being formed and destroyed all the time by very large forces. This happens very slowly over millions of years.

In the mountains, rainwater gets into the cracks in rocks. The water then expands as it freezes, and fragments of rocks are weathered (broken off). These fragments are then carried away, either by falling down the side of the mountain or by fast-flowing streams.

The fragments of rock have sharp edges. As they move, they rub against other rocks and this makes the edges more rounded.

The larger pieces of rock can only be carried by very fast-moving streams. Where the land becomes less steep and the stream flows more slowly, these large pieces fall to the bottom of the stream.

The smaller, lighter fragments of rock can be carried by much slower-flowing streams. Some are carried as far as estuaries and out into the open sea. Here they fall to the bottom of the sea as sediment and start the process of forming new sedimentary rocks. These may contain fossils. These sedimentary rocks may be forced upwards when the Earth's crust moves. Mount Everest was once at the bottom of the sea. We know this because fossils of sea organisms can be found at the top of the mountain.

The sedimentary rocks may also be forced down deeper into the Earth, where it is very hot. Here they are under pressure from all the rocks above them. The sedimentary rocks are changed into metamorphic rocks.

Metamorphic rocks may also be forced upwards by the movements of the Earth or forced downwards. If metamorphic rocks are forced deeper into the Earth, they melt and become magma. Magma is forced out of volcanoes when the pressure builds up, forming a mountain.

The cycle of rock destruction and formation starts again.

1 What is the name of the process, described in the information above, that causes pieces of rock to break off?

....

2 Give **two** other ways in which rocks may be worn away.

....

....

3 Name the force that causes the broken rock pieces to move.

....

4 What process causes the rocks to become smoother as they move?

....

5 Explain why the size of a fragment of rock determines where it ends up.

....

....

....

....

6 How does the distance a rock fragment travels affect its shape?

....

....

....

....

7 Suggest what could happen to Mount Everest over the next few million years.

....

....

....

....

....

....

8 Give **two** factors that are needed to change sedimentary rocks into metamorphic rocks.

....

....

9 Describe what happens to metamorphic rock that is forced upwards.

....

....

....

....

8.3 The fossil record of the horse

This challenge task relates to **8.9 The fossil record** from the Coursebook.

> In this challenge task, you will need to use information about horse fossils from a diagram and describe how the horse has changed over millions of years. You may want to do some additional research. You may also want to make notes on paper first before copying your answer into the workbook.

Many fossils of horses have been found in rocks. Some of these are about 55 million years old. From studying the many fossils, scientists have learnt how horses have changed over this time.

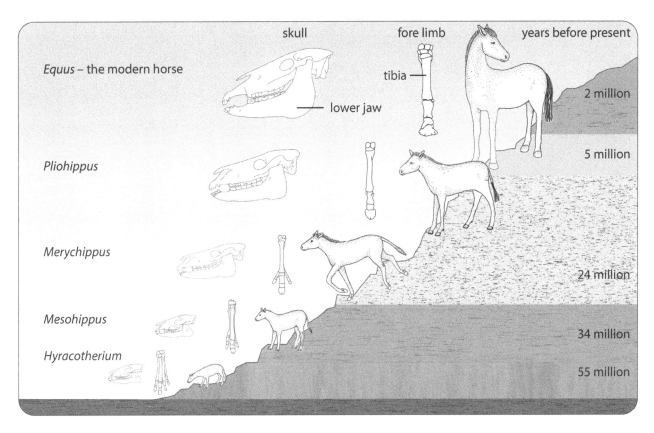

This diagram shows the fossils of horses that have been found at different levels in rocks. The deeper the rock, the older it is. The fossils show that horses have changed over millions of years.

1 Look carefully at the diagram. Use the information there, and any research that you do, to describe how the horse **has changed** over time and in what ways it **has not changed**.

> You need to consider any changes to the size of the whole animal, changes to the structure of the leg, and changes to the skull.
>
> Plan your description carefully.

9.1 Identifying forces

This challenge task relates to **9.1 Seeing forces**, **9.2 Forces big and small** and **9.3 Weight – the pull of gravity** from the Coursebook.

> In this challenge task, you will identify forces, including less obvious ones, and consider how forces act in everyday situations.

1 A book is at rest on a table. Describe, as fully as you can, the forces acting on the book.

....

....

....

2 Look at the diagram. Draw and label an arrow for each of these two forces on the diagram:

- The bow and arrow have weight, which is a force that acts downwards.

- Anna supports the bow and arrow with a lift force that acts upwards.

Now find **four** more forces. Draw and label an arrow for each of these forces on the diagram.

3 Explain the meaning of the notice on this bridge, in terms of forces.

> 2 tonnes = 2000 kg
>
> weight (N) = mass (kg) x 10
>
> Remember that kg is a unit of mass. Mass is **not** a force.

....

....

....

....

9.2 Friction and air resistance

This challenge task relates to **9.4 Friction – an important force** and **9.5 Air resistance** from the Coursebook.

> In this challenge task, you will describe when friction can be useful and when it can cause problems. You will also think about the variables in an investigation on air resistance.

1 Make a list of situations where friction is useful.

Make another list of situations where friction is unwanted.

Useful	Unwanted
....	....
....	....
....	....
....	....
....	....

A 'maglev' is a type of train. It uses magnets to lift the train off the track when it moves, so the train does **not** touch the ground.

2 Write down **one** advantage of a maglev train, compared with a normal train that touches the ground.

....

....

3 A train that does not touch the ground could be unsafe. Suggest **two** problems that would need to be solved for a maglev train to be safe.

....

....

....

....

Nor wants to investigate how air resistance affects some different model cars.

She ties a piece of light string to the front of each car, and the other end of the string to a forcemeter. The forcemeter is attached to a wooden block, which is clamped to the bench.

Nor then points a hairdryer at the front of the car and switches it on.

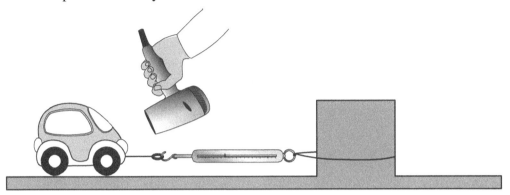

The model car will be blown backwards by the air from the hairdryer.

4 How will Nor be able to **measure** the air resistance using this equipment?

....

5 Nor is investigating how the type of model car affects the air resistance. Think about the variables in this experiment.

Tick the correct column of the table to show whether a variable should be **changed**, **kept the same**, **observed**, or would have **no effect**.

Variable	Changed?	Kept the same?	Observed?	No effect?
type of model car				
colour of the car				
speed setting of the hairdryer				
angle of the hairdryer				
distance from hairdryer to car				
reading on the newton meter				
type of surface				

6 Predict how the shape of the model car would affect the air resistance.

....

....

9.3 The speed of falling objects

This challenge task relates to **9.6 Patterns of falling** from the Coursebook.

> In this challenge task, you will plot and interpret a graph, then consider the variables in an experiment.

When you drop any object, it falls. As it falls, it speeds up because of gravity.

In theory, its speed should increase by about 10 m/s every second it falls. But that happens only if there is no air resistance.

Sam has found this table on the internet.

The table shows how the speed of a ball changes each second as it falls.

1 Plot a graph of these results. Put time on the x-axis and speed on the y-axis.

Time in s	Speed in m/s
0	0
1	9
2	17
3	24
4	26
5	26

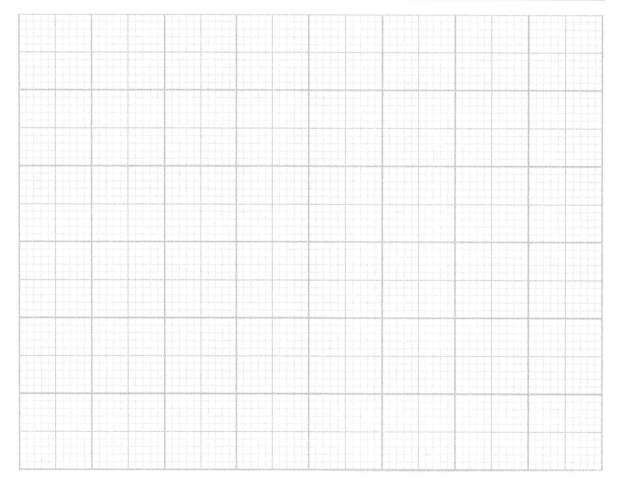

2 Describe, in as much detail as you can, what the graph shows about the movement of the ball and the forces on it in the **first three seconds**.

....

....

....

....

....

3 Sam says that the ball took four seconds to reach its maximum speed.

Explain why the ball reached a maximum speed and did **not** keep getting faster.

....

....

....

....

4 Sam predicts that different objects with the same mass will take different times to fall from a certain height.

Describe an investigation Sam can do to test this statement.

....

....

....

....

....

....

5 Sam drops an object and times how long it takes to fall. It takes 2.2 seconds.

He repeats this test and records a result of 3.5 seconds.

What should Sam do next? Explain your answer.

....

....

10.1 Investigating energy stores

This challenge task relates to **10.3 More energy stores** from the Coursebook.

> In this challenge task, you will describe how energy stores are
> used in different ways and how to investigate energy stores.

1 Complete the table by putting one tick beside each object to show the energy
store that makes it work.

Object	Battery	Coiled spring	Being moved to a height
playground swing			
mobile phone			
roller coaster			
wind-up toy			

2 For each energy store in the table, write down the **type** of energy that is stored.

a battery ....

b coiled spring ....

c being moved to a height ....

The energy store in a candle is the chemical energy in the wax.

The chemical energy is released when the candle is burned.

Not all types of wax used in candles are the same.

Elsa has two candles made from different types of wax.

Elsa wants to find out which of the two types of wax stores more energy.

She knows that she can burn the candles and use heat from the flame to heat water.

3 Plan an investigation using this method to find out which of the two types of wax stores more energy.

Remember to make it a fair test in every way possible.

....

....

....

....

....

....

....

....

....

....

....

....

....

....

....

....

....

10.2 Cooling down

This challenge task relates to **10.4 Thermal energy** from the Coursebook.

> In this challenge task, you will describe how thermal energy spreads out to the surroundings.

1 Read these statements about stored energy.

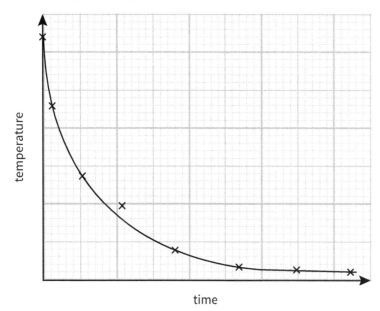

- The chemical energy in coal has been stored for millions of years and will not escape until the coal is burned.

- The thermal energy in a cup of hot tea will escape as the tea cools down.

- The gravitational potential energy stored in the water in the tank on top of this house will escape when the water is allowed to flow down to the house.

Which form of energy is the most difficult to store?
Tick **one** box.

chemical ☐

thermal ☐

gravitational potential ☐

To answer the next questions, look at this graph. It shows how the temperature of a hot liquid changes with time.

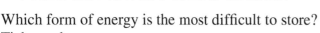

The results were taken from a thermometer placed in a beaker of hot water.

The water was stirred before the temperature was recorded.

Use the graph on the previous page to answer these questions.

2 Elsa and Jon each have a bowl of hot soup. Elsa's soup is much hotter than Jon's. Their teacher says that Elsa's soup will decrease in temperature faster than Jon's.

Is the teacher correct? Explain your answer.

....

....

....

....

3 Jon makes a prediction.

> The graph shows that the temperature of the soup will eventually stop decreasing

When will the temperature of the soup stop decreasing?
Tick **one** box.

when it is higher than the temperature of the room ☐

when it is the same as the temperature of the room ☐

when it is lower than the temperature of the room ☐

4 Draw a circle around any point on the graph that does **not** fit the pattern of the other results.

Suggest what could have happened to cause the result that you have circled.

....

....

10.3 Different ways of changing energy

This challenge task relates to **10.7 Energy changing form** from the Coursebook.

In this challenge task, you will learn more about how a battery works and describe different ways of changing energy.

When energy is transferred, it may be changed from one form into another form. Energy can be measured with the unit J.

Batteries contain chemical energy, which is only changed to electrical energy when they are put into a circuit.

Nor wants to find out more about how a battery works.

She finds some information on a website.

A battery, or dry cell, contains chemicals that react together to produce electricity.

As these chemicals that are in a battery react together, they produce other waste chemicals that slowly build up.

These waste chemicals slow down the production of electricity.

The chemical reaction will also get slower as the original chemicals will start to run out.

1 Use the information to describe why batteries eventually stop working.

....

....

....

2 Suggest why batteries of the same type that last longer are usually bigger.

....

....

Nor sees a radio for sale.

This radio works from electrical energy, but it does **not** use batteries and it does **not** need to be plugged into an electricity supply.

It has a handle that can be turned for one minute to make the radio work for 25 minutes. It works like a wind-up toy.

3 Suggest the energy transfers that happen in the radio, from being wound up to playing music.

....

....

....

....

....

4 A television is supplied with 1000 J of electrical energy.

400 J is transferred as light energy for the picture.

200 J is transferred as sound energy.

a Work out how much energy is **not** changed to light or sound.

Show your working and give the unit in your answer.

....

....

....

b Suggest the form of the energy that is **not** changed to light or sound.

Also suggest where it goes or what it is used for.

....

....

11.1 Moons around other planets

This challenge task relates to **11.6 A revolution in astronomy** from the Coursebook.

> In this challenge task, you will consider how observations are made.

In 1610, when looking at Jupiter through his telescope, Galileo saw four smaller objects close to the planet.

He thought they were stars, but each night they had moved slightly.

These are two of the drawings he made on two different nights.

The objects moved so slowly that their positions only changed noticeably after 24 hours. They always stayed close to the planet.

Galileo followed their movement and decided they were moons orbiting Jupiter.

1 Tick the box beside the method Galileo used to make this discovery.

listening to other scientists ☐   making observations ☐

laboratory experiment ☐   researching from books ☐

2 Using binoculars, Elsa sees the planet Jupiter and four smaller objects close to it.

Explain how Elsa could decide whether these smaller objects are the moons and **not** stars.

....

....

....

3 These moons are moving in circles around Jupiter, but from the Earth the moons appear to move only left and right.

On some clear nights when Elsa looks, she cannot see all of the four moons.

Suggest why some of the moons are not visible at certain times.

....

....

....

11.2 Discoveries in astronomy

This challenge task relates to **11.7 400 years of astronomy** from the Coursebook.

> In this challenge task, you will make conclusions about discoveries.

Until about 1780, only the six planets closest to the Sun were known.

1 List the six planets closest to the Sun, in order of increasing distance from the Sun.

....

....

2 In 1781, the astronomer William Herschel built a large telescope to observe the stars.

Suggest why some scientists, such as Herschel, need to build their own equipment rather than buying it.

....

....

....

....

3 When Herschel was using his telescope, he saw a new object that looked like a star. Every night, this object moved compared to the background of stars. He concluded it was a planet.

Suggest why Herschel concluded it was a planet and not a star.

....

....

4 The new object appeared to move more slowly than Saturn.

Explain why this made Herschel think that the new object was further away than Saturn.

....

....

5 The planet that Herschel discovered is now called Uranus.

Uranus takes 88 years to orbit the Sun.

Neptune is approximately **twice** as far away from the Sun as Uranus.

Predict how long it takes for Neptune to orbit the Sun ....

11.3 Probing space

This challenge task relates to **11.8 Journey into space** from the Coursebook.

> In this challenge task, you will **evaluate** modern methods for investigating space.

In 1977, a spacecraft called *Voyager 2* was launched from Earth. *Voyager 2* had no people on board. It is a type of spacecraft called an unmanned probe. Its job was to photograph planets and transmit the pictures back to Earth.

In 1986, *Voyager 2* passed close by Uranus and took some very detailed photographs of the planet.

1 Calculate, using the information above, how long *Voyager 2* took to get from Earth to Uranus.

....

2 Explain why *Voyager 2* took a long time to get to Uranus.

....

3 Modern cameras can take better quality photographs than was possible with cameras in 1986.

Suggest why the photographs taken by *Voyager 2* in 1986 showed **more** detail of Uranus than photographs taken from Earth today using modern cameras.

....

....

4 *Voyager 2* passed Neptune in 1989 and is now travelling further out into space. It is expected that we could still be receiving information from *Voyager 2* in the year 2025.

Suggest **two** reasons why we will eventually stop receiving information from *Voyager 2*.

....

....

....

....

5 Draw a large table with two columns. One column is for **advantages** and the other is for **disadvantages**.

Complete your table with the advantages and disadvantages of using an unmanned probe to photograph planets, compared with a spacecraft with people on board.

Try to think of at least **two** advantages and at least **two** disadvantages.